MENOR

CW00432910

Editorial Everest would like to thank you for purchasing this book. It
has been created by an extensive and complete publishing team
made up of photographers, illustrators and authors specialised in
the field of tourism, together with our modern cartography
department. Everest guarantees that the contents of this work
were completely up to date at the time of going to press, and we
would like to invite yoy to send us any information that helps us to
improve our publications, so that we may always offer
QUALITY TOURISM.

QUALITY
TOURISM
WITH
EVEREST

Please send your comments to:
Editorial Everest. Dpto. de Turismo
Apartado 339 – 24080 León (Spain)
Or e-mail them to us at turismo@everest.es

Editorial Management: Raquel López Varela

Editorial coordination: Eva María Fernández

Text: Miquel Ferrá i Martorell

Photographs: Francisco Sánchez

Diagrams: Mercedes Fernández

Cover design: Alfredo Anievas

Digital image processing: David Aller

Translation: EURO:TEXT

© EDITORIAL EVEREST, S. A.
Carretera León-La Coruña, km 5 - LEÓN
ISBN: 84-241-0611-3
Legal deposit: LE. 231-2006
Printed in Spain

EDITORIAL EVERGRÁFICAS, S. L.
Carretera León-La Coruña, km 5
LEÓN (Spain)

MENORCA

AN ISLAND OF GREEN, WHITE AND BLUE

An island of green, white and blue. This was how a poet once described it and he was not wrong. The island, the most northern of the Balearic archipelago, and the second largest in terms of surface area (701.84 km^2), has a prolific and vibrant history. In classical times, it was called *Meloussa* and *Nura,* and later, in Latin, *Minorca.* Today, it is one of the most important tourist destinations in the Mediterranean. Its archaeological and historical-artistic heritage makes it ideal for cultural visits and if we add to this the advantages of a mild climate and a marvellously diverse landscape, good road infrastructures, easy transport on urban and inter-urban buses, a hotel network of considerable professional prestige and interesting popular customs and festivals, as well as its unique and varied gastronomy, it is an attractive location for all.

Above, Barranc son Fideu. Below, Cala Morell.

A RICH NATURAL SETTING

The island was mainly formed during the Calcareous Miocene, whose horizontal strata constitute a uniform plain, at times monotonous, at times very rocky, which probably dates back to the time of the Alpine folding. In any case, the northern part is more humid and uneven, with Devonian and Jurassic rock structures. In contrast, on the southern coast many cliffs are to be found along a constant and even shore, whilst the rest of the coastline is more irregular, with many coves, ports, inlets, lagoons and wet areas. The terrain has few high points since, in general, the island is quite flat with only gentle hillocks. However, these low plains serve to give greater majesty to the small mountains that stand against the harsh north winds and cold. There may be few mountains but there exists a comparably rough landscape that is interrupted by clefts, or gullies, which are turned into orchards when streams flow through them.

Seagull.

Iberian wall lizard.

A MAINLY MILD CLIMATE

The climate of Minorca is typically Mediterranean, mild and damp yet also sunny. Its only enemy is the cold and dry mistral or north wind, locally known as the "tramontana", which blows from the coasts of the Gulf of Lion. The temperatures are pleasant and generally vary between 8 and 12 °C in winter and an average of 25 °C in the summer months. The flora has adapted to this climate and is rich and diverse. It ranges from modest scorpion broom, wild asparagus and soothing rosemary through to Holm oaks, olive and carob trees and pines (the most common species), as well as myrtle, white heather, common broom and many other plants which form a vegetation which rivals the large grazing meadows. As far as fauna is concerned, some small mammals are to be found in this green setting, the survival of a wild microcosmos, in which there is no shortage of rabbits, hares, hedgehogs, bats and pine martens which compete with thousands of birds such as kites, falcons, ospreys, barn owls, little owls, partridges, turtledoves, seagulls, crows, thrushes and nightingales. Perhaps the least numerous branch of this generally indigenous fauna would be that of reptiles, although there are some tortoises, snakes and lizards which are harmless to man and are included in the lists of protected species.

Above, Cala'n Porter. Below, meadows.

LIVING HISTORY

Talking of mankind, the first settlers reached Minorca around 4000 years before Christ. They were a peaceful, cave-dwelling people who farmed the land, kept cattle and were experts in bronze work. During the second phase, towards the year 1200 before Christ, the island was inhabited by a group of people who are thought to have come from the Eastern Mediterranean and became the real "Balearics" or representatives of what has been called the "Talayotic Culture" due to their Cyclopean constructions in the shape of towers, locally called "talayots" or watchtowers. Other typical features of proto-historic Minorca include its "navetas", funerary monuments which take the shape of an upturned vessel, and its unique megalithic "taulas", two large rectangular stones whose three-dimensional appearance reminds us of a giant table or the letter T, when in profile. The "taulas" have, as a result, been subject to various interpretations. Some archaeologists believe that they are nothing more than constructive elements similar to pillars, whilst others consider them to have a religious-funerary significance. They may have been altars upon which corpses were laid or the pulpit from which priests addressed the people. Alternatively,

Above and below, detail and panoramic view of a "naveta" in Ciutadella.

8

Talaiot de Torrellonet Vell.

they may have been a stylised representation of a bull's head, since Balearic sling-fighters worshipped the bull before later adopting Mars, God of War, as their special protector during the Punic wars and other military campaigns of the ancient world. The best conserved "taulas" are those of Trepucó, Talatí, Torralba d'En Salort, Torreta de Tramuntana, Na Comerma, Torre Trencaday and Torre Llafuda, although there exist at least a dozen more which have no traditional name. Besides this highly original historical wealth, there also exist around thirty "navetas" and half a dozen spectacular "talayots", such as those of Torre d'En Gaumes, Alcaidús and Son Catlar. To this list, we must add the cave shrine of Cales Coves and around 60 caves which were inhabited as early as the second millennium of the Bronze Age, all of which are of great interest to history lovers. Yet more frequent are the dolmens,

megalithic monuments formed by a horizontal slab laid upon vertical blocks. Three such sites have been identified in Sa Comerma de Sa Garita, Montple and Alcaidus. In the year 123 before Christ, General Quintus Cecilius Metelus conquered the archipelago and the latter came to form part of the political and social life of Rome. According to Latin chroniclers, Minorca possessed three cities at the time: Mago (Maó), Iamo (Ciutadella) and Sanicera (Sanitja). Christianity reached the archipelago in the 3rd century and just one hundred years later, at the time of Bishop Severus, it was already well-rooted in popular culture. Good testimony to this is provided by the remains of Paleochristian basilicas that are to be found in Cap de Fornells, Illa del Rei, Fornás de Torrelló and Son Bou. The next step in the island's history brings us to the Muslim invasion and centuries of domination which began at the start of the 10th century. Muslim Minorca was governed by an Almojarife in Madina-Menurqa, modern-day Ciutadella, and was divided into four administrative regions ruled by "sahibs": Hasmaljuda, Banu-Said, Banu-Fabin and Alscaions. This long period left behind many fortresses, such as the ruins of Santa Águeda Castle, the remains of a tower within the bell tower of the Cathedral of Cuitadella and the Puente del General bridge inside the walled enclosure of Maó, as well as numismatics, ceramics, epigraphy and many place names such as Binicossitx, Binimassó, Albranca, Binigaus, Biniseguí, Alfurinet and Binixebró.

This situation changed for good when, after the Moors of Minorca had been feudatories of Jaime I The Conqueror and his successors since 1230, the island was militarily occupied, following fierce fighting, by Alfonso III, King of Aragon, in 1286. As part of the Catalan-Aragonese kingdom, it would later suffer the ups and downs of the aforesaid monarchy in the history of Spain. However, certain events in local history were to have a decisive and dramatic effect on all of the island's inhabitants. During the 16th and 17th centuries, the Turkish threatened the island with landings in Maó and Ciutadella in 1535 and 1558, respectively, which on both occasions led to pillaging and the taking of men, women and children as slaves.

However, it was the 18th century that would bring interesting and unexpected events to the island, almost all of them as a consequence of the Spanish War of Succession between the Bourbons and the Hapsburgs (1700-1714). In order to compensate the military

Talatí de Dalt

Taula de Torralba.

efforts undertaken in its alliance with the Archduke of Austria, England occupied Gibraltar and Minorca, a masterly move based on the advantages of possessing two of the most strategic points in the Mediterranean. The British presence in Minorca continued for almost a century and was long enough to have an influence on its customs and even its idiosyncrasies. It lasted from 1708 to 1802, with the exception of the periods 1756-1763 (French sovereignty) and 1782-98 (reincorporation within Spain). Many important figures lived during this period, as indicated by the Maó writer Llorenç Lafuente (1881-1936): Stanhope, Blakeney, Duke Richelieu, Murray, Draper, Duke Crillon, Count Cifuentes and Captain General Vives, but none like the British Governor Richard Kane, of whom Minorca holds fond memories. This Irishman, who guided the island's destiny for over two decades, was peace-loving, intelligent and a great civil servant. As the

Taula de Trepucó.

writer Josep Pla once said, it would be a long task to list the details of his good management: he restored law and order, put an end to banditry, suppressed the Inquisition, maintained discipline at the heart of the garrisons, efficiently negotiated with the clergy, moralised customs, opened the first road from Maó to Ciutadella (Kane Road), reorganised the legal system, moved the capital to Maó in order to fully develop its port, modernised the city, passed legislation regarding the local currency, imported seeds, plants and tree species, created orchards, introduced sulla as a forage crop, promoted boat construction and improved the island's livestock. The Amiens Treaty returned Minorca to the Spanish Crown, once and for all. John Armstrong, an engineer who served the British Monarchy in Minorca, left us *The History of the Island of Menorca*, published in Chelsea in 1752, which contains many references describing the island as it was in the 18th century. The British influence upon Minorca can still be

Above, Torre Llafuda. Below, Torre d'En Gaumes.

observed in certain architectural details, such as neoclassical pediments or so-called "sash" windows. The English period left behind several dozen words in the Catalan language of the Minorcans, various children's games, snippets of songs, folk dances, traditional clothing and recipes which form part of its rich gastronomy. Another curious phenomenon was the emigration of Minorcans to Florida, at a time when it formed part of English America. This expedition, led by a man called Turnbull, founded the city of New Smirna, repopulated that of San Agustín and has been recreated in North American literature, particularly in the novels of Frank G. Slaughter (Storm Haven).

During the War of Independence (1808-1814), Spain joined forces with Great Britain in its fight against Napoleon and once again allowed the port of Maó to become an English navel base, with around 10,000 seamen living amongst the civil population. Later, during the early decades of the 19th century, the United States of America found itself fighting the corsairs of Libya and Algiers, in order to protect its commercial fleet in the Mediterranean, and used the Maó naval base for its war squadron, which was led by the famous frigate "Constitution". This vessel was the best of its time, weighing 2200 tonnes, and was launched in 1797 and captained by William Baimbridge. Incidentally, the United States' Admiral David Farragut (1801-1870), who made a name for himself with the northern forces during the North American Civil War, was the son of a Minorcan pioneer. In 1867, as Chief of the North American squadron in Europe, he decided to visit Ciutadella in order to see the land of his ancestors and was given the welcome of a local hero.

Towards the second half of the 19th century, many Minorcans emigrated to French Algeria and formed an important part of its European population. Towards 1882, there

The ruins of Santa Águeda Castle.

were a total of 24,960 Minorcans living there, including the grandparents of the great French writer Albert Camus (1913-1960). Indeed, one of its towns, Fort de l'Eau, was almost entirely Minorcan.

During the Civil War, Minorca was loyal to the Republic, unlike Mallorca, which supported the military uprising right from the start. Incidents such as the submarine mail service between Minorca and Barcelona, immortalised in stamps, cannot fail to awaken our curiosity.

Towards the end of the 1950's and during the decade of the 1960's, Minorca began to witness a growth in its tourist economy, which complemented its industrial activities. In the year 1993, the island requested UNESCO classification as a Biosphere Reserve, a title which provides world-wide recognition and

corresponds to its assets of 700 km^2 of thriving natural life, 200 kilometres of coastline, plentiful farming land and a harmonious future for man and the environment.

A HERITAGE OF HISTORICAL MONUMENTS

La Rada de Maó

With its small islands, "La Rada de Maó" forms an area of historical interest. The island of **Lazareto** has neoclassical buildings which were used, in the past, to impose quarantine upon people, ships and merchandise that arrived from locations in which contagious diseases were present. It possesses courtyards, a chapel, storerooms, bedrooms and other forms of accommodation which take us back to the 18th century. Then we have

Paleochristian basilica of Son Bou.

Above, view of the "Cementerio Inglés". Below, La Mola Fortress.

Isla del Rey ("Island of the King"), whose name refers to the fact that Alfonso III disembarked there during the Christian Reconquest. Here, there stands a hospital which is known by the English name of "Bloody Island", a huge 18th century building, also neoclassical in style, which was constructed for the British sailors of the time. The **island of Pinto** is linked to the mainland by a bridge and also features 18th century-style buildings, crowned by clock towers - old storehouses, offices, shipyards and workshops stand upon a circular quay structure which also dates back to the time of the "jans" (the Minorcan term used in the past to refer to the English). Back on dry land, there are emblematic places such as the **Granja de San Antonio,** or **Golden Farm,** a sienna and white-coloured neoclassical colonial building, on the top of a hill, in which it is said that Admiral Horatio Nelson once stayed

and that even Lady Hamilton may have once rested, during a stop-over between London and Naples. Not far from there, down in a small cove surrounded by white walls, stands the **Cementerio Inglés** ("English Cemetery") with tombs of English and North American sailors from the end of the 18th and start of the 19th century.

There are also fortresses: **La Mola,** on the cape of the same name, was built in the time of Isabel II upon what had once been the stronghold of Queen Ana; the remains of the **Fort of San Felipe** and **San Felipet,** with its panes and mysterious passageways and mines; the **Fort of Marlboroug,** a name which became "Mambrú" in old children's songs and refers to John Churchill, Duke of Marlborough (1650-1722), the English General who led the British troops during the Spanish War of Succession, another Vauban-style enclosure for artillery.

Es Castell. Above, view.
Left, parade ground.

Es Castell is the name given to another town (formerly Villacarlos) which was built by the British, under the name of George Town, with perfectly straight streets and a large parade ground in the centre where the barracks of the English garrison were once located. In turn, the French, who dominated the island for a shorter period, founded the town of **Saint-Louis** or **San Luís**, with a church whose façade displays a commemorative plaque. If we leave the inlet behind us, we enter

Panoramic view o
Es Castel

Maó. Gate of San Roque.

Maó. Above, Town Hall façade.
Right, Casa Mir (modernist building).

he urban fabric of **Maó** and can visit
he remains of its old medieval
walls, such as the **arch** or **gate of**
San Roque, flanked by two 16th
century towers, all of which reveal a
ivil Gothic style. Next we come to
he **Town Hall,** in Constitution
Square, which dates back to the 17th
entury and was beautifully modified
o give it a neoclassical style in the
8th century. A particularly interesting
eature of its façade is the watch
ower that was brought from
England by Governor Kane. Our
ultural tour also takes us to **Can**
Mercadel, a building which follows
he same style as the last and is
urrently used as a library, archive
ffice and museum, with Mayan,
aztec, Talayotic and Roman objects.
along similarly pedagogical lines, we
ave the **Scientific and Literary**
Cultural Centre, with an important
brary covering Minorcan issues,
eramics collections from the 16th

and 17th centuries and an interesting exhibition of birds, molluscs and algae. The religious buildings of interest include the **Church of Santa María** and the **Church and Convent of San Francisco.** The first dates from the 18th century and is located in the aforementioned Constitution Square, in the centre of the city. It has one single neoclassical nave and side chapels in the same style. Its most outstanding feature is a monumental organ with four keyboards and over three thousand tubes which was made by the Swiss craftsman Kiburz in 1810. This church contains the tomb of Count Lannion, the French governor who died in Maó in 1762, and that of Marques Frémeur, who died in the same city in 1759.

22

View of Maó
In the background
Church of Santa María

Maó. Above, el Carmen Church. Below, Church of San Francisco.

Double page overleaf, panoramic view of Maó port.

The Church of San Francisco is the modern-day location of the **Museum of Minorca,** a reconstruction which also dates back to the 18th century, has just one nave and is accessed via a medieval Romanesque-style doorway. The route may also include the **el Carmen Church** which dates from 1751. It has been fully restored and contains three naves and a choir that is preceded by a transept dome. Behind the altar, in a lady chapel, stands a highly venerated 18th century Virgin, patron of sailors. To

the left of this church stands the former conventual cloisters. However, without doubt, the liveliest part of the city is to be found in the streets of Calle Hannover, with its old buildings full of Anglo-Saxon details, and Paseo del Doctor Orfila, with a monument to this scholar marking the house in which he was born. We must remember that Mateo José Buenaventura Orfil (Maó, 1787 – Paris, 1853), a Minorcan chemist and doctor who adopted French nationality and wrote the *"Treaty on poisons extracted from the mineral, plant and animal kingdoms or general toxicology"* (1813-1815), achieved extraordinary prestige as a result of his research. Other generally busy or interesting parts of the town include the Explanada and Calle del Cos de Gracia, which reminds one of the equestrian festival dedicated to Nuestra Señora de Gracia, the patron of Maó. Perhaps the most interesting streets of all are Calle de San Jorge and Avenida de los Mártires del Atlante.

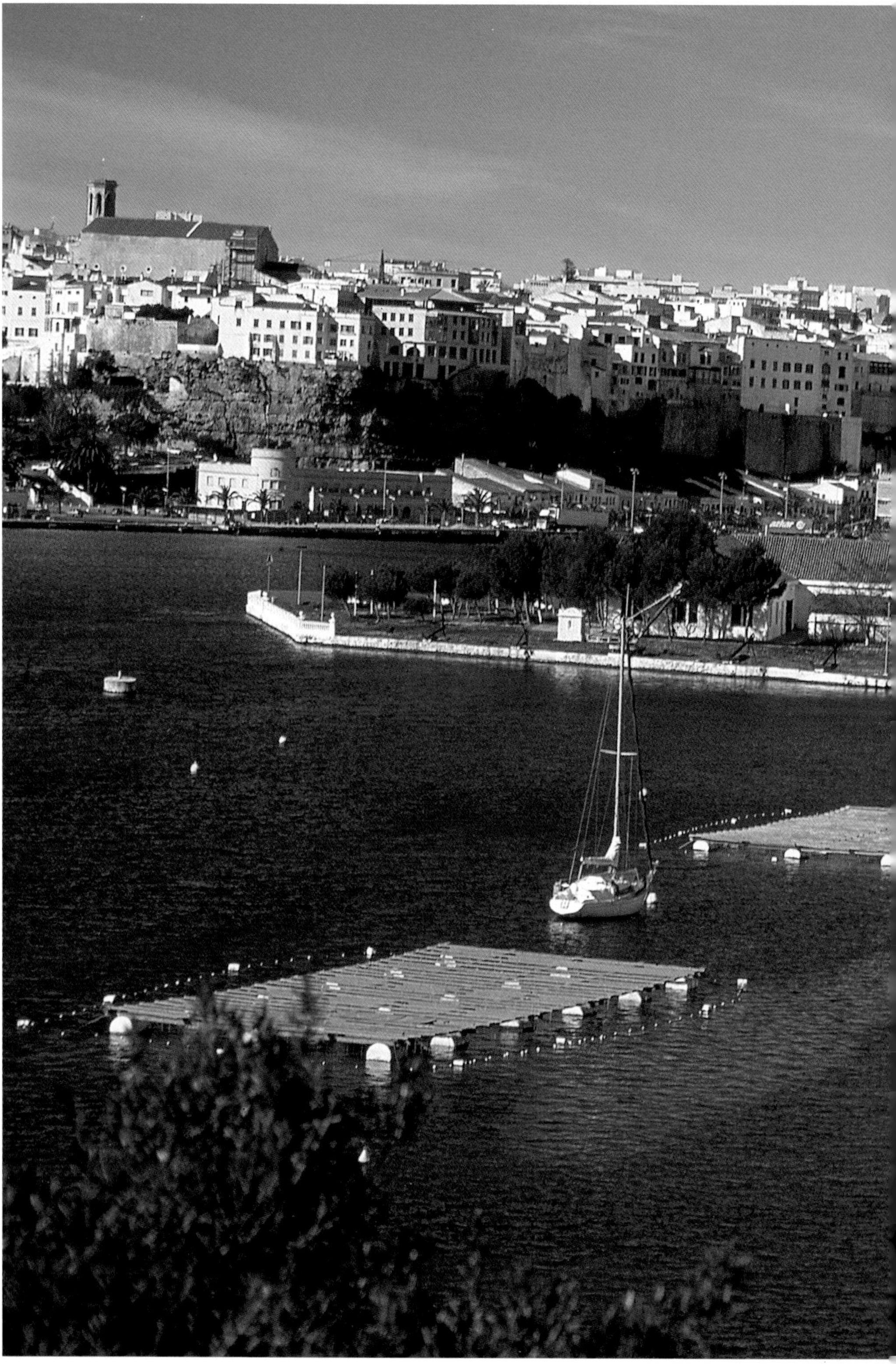

Majestic Ciutadella

Founded, like Maó, by the Phoenicians, Ciutadella is the island's former capital and home to its bishopric. Built next to a small estuary which flows out from the west coast, it is an old city of whose walls only a few bastions remain to dominate the port. It is a highly evocative place of arcaded alleyways, eighteenth-century mansions, aristocratic palaces displaying old coats of arms in the relief of their façades and courtyards and balconies with baroque details. We can admire the 18th century **Saura Palace** with its beautiful doorway crowned by windows with attic mouldings and large carved eaves. We may also gaze at the loggia of the **Torresaura and Vigo houses,** and the structure of Ca'n Esquella, inside which there is a paved area with an *opus espicatum,* a form of Roman bonding in the shape of a fishbone, which gave the

house its name. The **Town Hall** stands in Born Square, where some of the knightly festivals of San Juan are held. It occupies what was once the **Real Alcázar** (Moorish Palace) and later the Governor's residence, and contains a Gothic hall, restored in 1897 in accordance with the post-romantic tendencies of the time. Special mention must be given to the **Cathedral,** the former Church of Santa María, the Bishop's cathedra since 1795 and a basilica since 1953. Its construction began in 1362, upon a former mosque, and some claim that the remains of the minaret are visible in the bell tower. As is true of a good many monuments on the island, the 18th century façade is neoclassical, with a Corinthian gateway and a balustrade dating from 1814 which crowns the building. Its interior consists of one single nave, divided into six rib sections with side chapels. It suffered a fire during the attack of the Berber pirates of Mustafá Piali in 1558.

Ciutadella Town Hall

Ciutadella. Cathedral façade.

It conserves a bishop's throne, a choir which was restored in 1942 and altarpieces of undeniable value and good taste. In the centre of Born Square there stands an **obelisk** which commemorates "the year of misfortune", a phrase commonly used to refer to the year 1558, when the Turkish navy disembarked in the city and took many of its inhabitants (men, women and children) to Constantinople to serve as slaves. Also of great interest is the **Church of San Francisco,** a 13th century building that was reconstructed in the 16th century but maintains a Gothic nave, to which renaissance elements were added, and the

Ciutadella. Above, Born Square. Below, ses Voltes.

Church of Roser, with a baroque façade and a small interior structure consisting of a single nave. The former **Convent of San Agustín** houses an **Archaeological Museum** and contains a good collection of prehistoric pieces from the island of Rincones and relics that were described with post-romantic irony by the local scholar Joan Benejam Vives in 1909: "I shall tell of times when women spun and men wove; when people wore clothes of medium wool and light headscarfs, short trousers and buckled shoes; times of friars and administrators, of knights and servants, of ghosts and witches and all the rest."

Ciutadella. Right, windmill.
Below, panoramic view of port.

Ciutadella. Above, Sant Nicolau. Below, Sant Joan.

Particularly charming towns and villages

The range is wide and varied. **Villacarlos, George-Town** or **Es Castell,** whose folkloric "ball d'Escòcia" ("Scottish dance") contains a Catalan-British symbiosis in honour of its historical role as the residential and military barracks that were founded by the English in the 18th century. **Cala de Sant Esteve,** with its fishing population. The white town of **San Luís,** founded in 1761 by the Quartermaster General Causan, under the French government of Count Lannion, whose church displays a commemorative plaque from the period, with picturesque windmills in the surrounding area. **Cala Alcaufar,** with a shrine that is dedicated to San Esteban and conserves the saint's remains which were brought from Palestine in 417. **Cala Punta Prima,** with a beautiful view of the

Cala de Sant Esteve. Above, D'en Penjant. Below, general view.

San Luís.
Above, view of town.
Left, windmill.

San Luís. Cala Alcaufar.

Left, Cala Benisafuller
Below and overleaf,
two views of Binibeca

island of Aire. **Cala Binisafuller** and **Cala Binibeca,** two oases of peace on a welcoming coast. **Cala Mesquida,** with its 14th century tower and well-sheltered beach. **La Albufera,** with its aquatic birds and rich fishing grounds. **El Grao,** with its splendid beach and beautiful views of En Colom island. **San Clemente,** with its interesting racecourse and the nearby Talatí archaeological site. **Cala Coves,** with its sensational cliffs and troglodyte dwellings or ancient burial chambers excavated into the rock. **Alaior,** the Montpellier of Minorca, with the Parish Church of Santa Eulalia and also the Church of San Diego, with a beautiful plateresque door. **Mercadal,** at the foot of **Monte Toro** ("Mount Bull"), the sanctuary of a black Virgin, according to druid tradition, related to the legend of bull worship which has also appeared in parts of Southern France. **Fornells,** with a church dedicated to San Antonio Abad and a typical fishing village. **Ferreries,** a picturesque hamlet which was once a town of blacksmiths, according to popular history, and whose closest mountain is called Enclusa ("Anvil" in Catalan). **Cala Santandría,** a spa with a beautiful beach. And many others, far too numerous to list here.

Cala Mesquida.

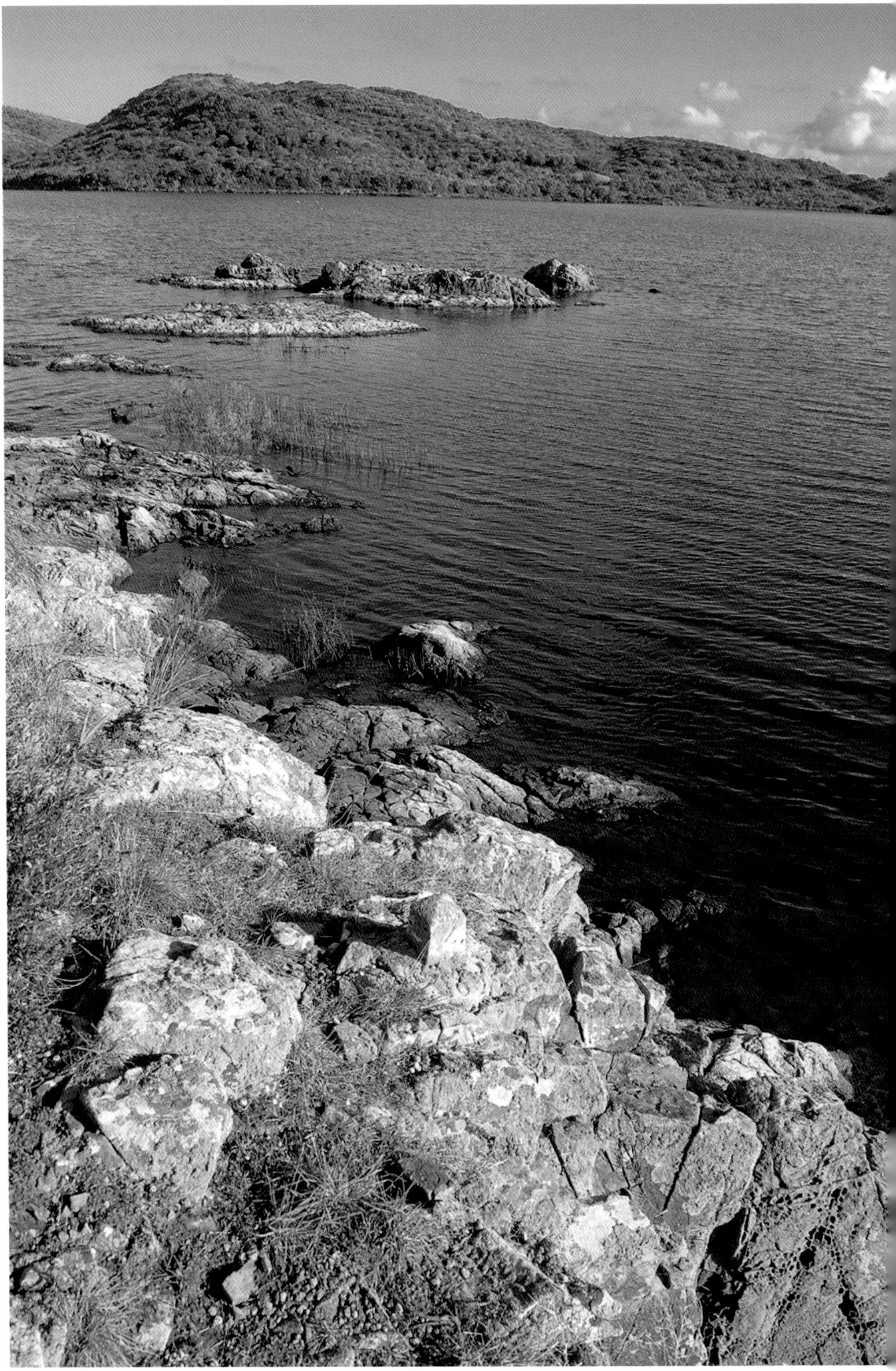

Different views of La Albufera.

Left, entrance to the sanctuary of Monte Toro.
Below, panoramic view of Monte Toro.
Overleaf, view of Ferreries.

A RICH AND VARIED GASTRONOMY

Minorcan gastronomy links the region's natural resources with its historical influences and has created, for one reason or another, a select, varied and truly unique cuisine which ranges from remnants of the period of Arab control, such as the dessert called "cuscussó", to modern sea fish stew, baked apples (Kane style) and fish served with a sauce that the French exported, under the name of "mayonnaise", to the rest of Europe and even Russia, in the times of Napoleon. Besides the "supreme" dishes of lobster or clam stew, the menu also offers simple broths such as "oliaigua" (olive oil and vegetable soup) and more elaborate recipes such as rice with lobster and rabbit. Pork meat is put to good use in dishes such as baked rice, Spanish omelette with "carn i xulla" (a

delicious pork sausage made on the island), swordfish with bacon and Minorcan-style meatballs. Perhaps seafood products predominate in the island's most original dishes, such as baked seabream, red mullet in liver sauce, cod fritters and stuffed moray eel. The meat dishes are equally worthy, due to their meticulous and traditional preparation, and it is only fair to

Overleaf, duck i
olive sauce

Above, lobster stew
Below, "ensaimada"

mention the lamb's trotter croquettes, cold cuts of pork or rabbit loin, liver paté, stuffed leg of lamb, meat pie, duck in olive sauce, stuffed sweet turkey, beef trotter casserole and garlic and parsley poultry stew. The island is also a land of excellent pickles, particularly capers in vinegar, wild olives and tinned tomatoes in oil or water. We cannot finish without mentioning the appetising dessert specialities such as the stuffed pastry parcels called "cocarrois", some of which are so original that they are filled with wild chicory. We must conclude by saying that the four most outstanding products are, by any reckoning, the universally recognised "Mahonés" cheese, the gin which is distilled according to 18th century English formulae, the aforementioned "carn i xulla" and "ensaimada" pastries, which are shared with Mallorca, Ibiza and Formentera. At Christmas, it is traditional to drink "calent" (mulled wine with sugar and cinnamon), at christenings, rose liqueur (probably inherited from the Greeks that lived on the island in the 18th century, like the Alexians and other rich merchant families) and, at any other celebration, Maó gin.

Minorca, therefore, offers a simple and generous welcome. Visitors are treated naturally and the island has maintained a certain eighteenth-century chivalry in the ways of its people. They are fond of their traditions whilst being open to industrial progress, craftspeople and artists. When we leave Minorca, we may choose to take with us some jewellery, maybe a model ship inspired in the times when the port of Maó gave refuge to a thousand frigates, perhaps some of the shoes that have turned Alaior and other towns into examples of model shoemaking and also a pair of the traditional sandals that have become popular among today's youth and date back to the time of the Almogavars.